The Statue of Liberty:
A Gift from France

by Carol Talley

Scott Foresman
is an imprint of

Glenview, Illinois • Boston, Massachusetts • Chandler, Arizona
Upper Saddle River, New Jersey

Every effort has been made to secure permission and provide appropriate credit for photographic material. The publisher deeply regrets any omission and pledges to correct errors called to its attention in subsequent editions.

Unless otherwise acknowledged, all photographs are the property of Scott Foresman, a division of Pearson Education.

Photo locators denoted as follows: Top (T), Center (C), Bottom (B), Left (L), Right (R), Background (Bkgd)

Opener ©Museum of the City of New York/CORBIS; 1 ©Bettmann/CORBIS; 3(T) ©Bettmann/CORBIS; 3(B) ©PoodlesRock/CORBIS; 4 ©Leonard de Selva/CORBIS; 5(T) ©Leonard de Selva/CORBIS; 5(B) ©Michael Maslan Historic Photographs/CORBIS; 6(T) ©Bettmann/CORBIS; 6(B) ©CORBIS; 7 ©Lance Nelson/CORBIS; 8 ©CORBIS; 9 ©CORBIS; 10(T) ©CORBIS; 10(B) ©CORBIS; 11 ©Hulton Archive/Getty Images; 12 ©Museum of the City of New York/CORBIS:

ISBN 13: 978-0-328-51419-9
ISBN 10:   0-328-51419-5

3 4 5 6 7 8 9 10 V0N4 13 12 11 10

The Statue of Liberty is on Liberty Island in New York Harbor.

The statue was a gift from the people of France to honor the friendship between our nations. It is a symbol of freedom.

The statue was made in Paris and then shipped to the United States.

What was Paris like in the 1880s when the statue was being built? Let's take a look around the city.

The river Seine runs through the center of Paris. Famous artists worked on its Left Bank. The Cathedral of Notre Dame is on an island in the Seine.

Paris around 1883

On the Right Bank, you could stroll under the Arc de Triomphe.

As you walked through Paris, you could look down narrow, crooked streets. Houses there are hundreds of years old.

The building of the Cathedral of Notre Dame began in 1163. It was not finished until 1345.

Frederic Auguste Bartholdi

Bartholdi's workshop

On a Sunday afternoon in 1883, you might see Parisians visiting the sculptor Frederic Auguste Bartholdi's workshop. He was the artist who created the Statue of Liberty. He made models of every part of the statue, including the crown and tablet, before building it.

The sculptor then hired an engineer named Alexandre Gustave Eiffel. He had designed the Eiffel Tower. Bartholdi asked Eiffel to design the inside framework that would support the statue.

Bartholdi completed the Statue of Liberty in June, 1884.

The Eiffel Tower is a popular landmark in Paris.

The Statue of Liberty was shipped to the United States. More than 200 crates carried all 350 parts of the statue. It took engineers four months to reassemble the statue on Bedloe's Island in New York Harbor. In 1960 the island was renamed Liberty Island.

New York City around 1884

What was New York City like in **1886**?
At night, the city was ablaze with light.

One of the most amazing sights you could see was the new Brooklyn Bridge. It was the longest suspension bridge in the world in 1886.

The Brooklyn Bridge

More than half of all New Yorkers lived in the Lower East Side in the 1880s. They were mostly immigrants who came to the United States to build better lives.

Immigrants lived in crowded conditions.

Some New Yorkers were rich and lived in mansions.

New Yorkers gather at Central Park to hear concerts.

Last of all, let's visit Central Park in the 1880s. It was a summer evening. Thousands of New Yorkers—rich and poor—had come to hear a free band concert.

11

On October 28, 1886, the Statue of Liberty was unveiled. Thousands of New Yorkers watched the unforgettable sight.

Since that day, millions of people have been welcomed to the United States by the light of Liberty's torch.

"Liberty Enlightening the World" by Edward Moran, 1886. ©Museum of the City of New York.